Flowers
of the World

Copyright © 2021 Akudo U Ehirim All rights reserved.
First paperback edition printed 2021 in the
United Kingdom
A catalogue record for this book is available from
the British Library.
ISBN 978-1-913455-30-9
No part of this book shall be reproduced or transmitted in
any form or by any means,
electronic or mechanical, including photocopying,
recording, or by any information retrieval
system without written permission of the publisher.
Published by Scribblecity Publications
Printed in Great Britain
Although every precaution has been taken in the
preparation of this book, the publisher and
author assume no responsibility for errors or omissions.
Neither is any liability assumed for
damages resulting from the use of this information
contained herein.
Illustrated by Omerbia Aja-Nwachuku.

Dedicated to the children of the world

We are **children**, children of the world, just like flowers, we are **flowers** of the world.

We are **different,** different in some ways, just like **flowers**, we are **similar** in most ways

Just like flowers, we come in multiple **colors**, colors of **beauty** that make the world rich.

Just like flowers, we come in multiple **shapes**, shapes that are **different** but come in **perfect** form.

Some of us are like **Tulips** that **bloom** in the springtime, Tulips that are yellow and **gorgeous** as can be.

Some of us are like the **Cactus** that bloom during the day, and just like the Cactus, they shut down too at night.

Some of us are like **peonies,** pink and **nice** to see.

Some of us are like **Daisies**, white, fresh and **young**.

Some of us grow where it is **wet**, while some of us **grow** in **dry** places. No matter where we grow or live, we are here to **thrive**.

Some of us are like **pansies**, **short**, and we spread around. Just like a Pansy, we **spread** everywhere.

Some of us are **small** in size, but we are very **cute**.

Some of us are like the **grass**, beautiful and **green**.

S ome of us are like **wild** flowers, full of **life** and **fun.** We are wild for everything we know, and **learning** too.

Some of us are like **weeds**, **special** and must be handled with **care**.

Some of us are like **Snapdragons**, **tall** and **beautifully** made.

Just like flowers, we all come with **different smells,** smells that are **lovely**, **sharp** and **good** to keep.

We belong to **different families** but we are **loved** by all.

Some of us are like **Roses**, red, pink and **sweet**. A **perfect** gift for everyone, and every Mom too.

Some of us are like **zinnias**, **pretty**, **cute** and **bold**.

Some of us are like **Hibiscus**, with colors of the rainbow. **Colors** that make you who you are.

Some of us are like **flowers** put in different **vases**, just like flowers, we belong to different **homes**.

Children of the world we are **everywhere.**
Just like flowers, we are everywhere.

Some of us come from the **same** family,
yet **different** in all ways.

Different in all the ways that count, yet we are still the **same**.

Some are like **seeds**, they make you work so hard. But in the end, it's **worth** the **time** and **effort**.

Some of us are like **Marigolds**, round and orange in color.

Unique and **special,** we are all the **same**. Just like the flowers.

We are **children** of the **world**.

www.ingramcontent.com/pod-product-compliance
Lightning Source LLC
Chambersburg PA
CBHW042000080526
44588CB00021B/2819